HONESTY

The newspaper machine owner is dependent on people's honesty.

HONESTY

Vana Earle

THE ROSEN PUBLISHING GROUP, INC.

NEW YORK

Published in 1990 by The Rosen Publishing Group, Inc.
29 East 21st Street, New York, NY 10010.

First Edition
Copyright 1990 by The Rosen Publishing Group, Inc.

Printed in Canada
Bound in the United States of America

Library of Congress Cataloging-in-Publication Data

Earle, Vana.
    Honesty / Vana Earle.
    (The Values library)
    Includes bibliographical references.
    Index.
    Summary: Defines honesty and discusses its importance in life.
    ISBN 0-8239-1109-8
    1. Honesty—Juvenile literature. [1. Honesty.   2. Conduct of
life.]   I. Title.   II. Series.
BJ1533.H7E37   1990   89-48773
179'.9—dc20   CIP
                                                                    AC

C O N T E N T S

Introduction THE IMPORTANCE OF
HONESTY   6

Chapter One TRUTH AND HONESTY   9

Chapter Two HONESTY IS THE BEST
POLICY   15

Chapter Three BE HONEST WITH YOURSELF   25

Chapter Four GOSSIPS, TATTLETALES, AND
LITTLE WHITE LIES   33

Chapter Five HONESTY AT WORK   43

Chapter Six ARE YOU AN HONEST
PERSON?   51

Glossary-Explaining New Words   60

For Further Reading   61

Index   63

THE IMPORTANCE OF HONESTY

HONESTY HAS AN IMPORTANT PLACE IN EVERYONE'S LIFE. We learn about honesty so early in life that we cannot remember first hearing about it. As we grow up, we learn about the many ways that honesty is part of dealing with others. It is also part of understanding ourselves.

Unlike other personal values, honesty is sometimes a matter of legal as well as personal importance. Compassion (caring about other people and what happens to them), for example, is important in understanding and getting along with others. But no one goes to jail for not having compassion. Lack of honesty, however, is a serious matter.

One way honesty is defined is "not lying, not cheating, not stealing." Stealing is against the law. To protect the personal property of others, those who steal can be tried in the courts. If found guilty they can be put in jail. Cheating can carry a stiff penalty, too. If a student cheats on a test, he or she can fail a course or be suspended from school.

Lying can be dangerous also. Many times we lie with the best of reasons. We do not want to hurt someone's feelings when they ask for our opinion. Or we lie about something that doesn't really matter to anyone but us. Sometimes a woman wants to seem young and doesn't want to tell her real age. But lying about something important can be a very different matter. If someone lies to the police to protect a friend, they are committing a crime. When someone does it in court it is called perjury. Perjury is telling a lie when you are sworn to tell the truth. Someone who commits perjury can be put in jail by a judge.

Other definitions of honesty include "not taking unfair advantage," and "being honorable." There are other ideas about honesty that are not in the dictionary. Being honest with yourself, and being honest with other people, are important tools for getting along in this world. We will talk about all of these things. You will see how they are important to you.

The story of young George Washington and the cherry tree is an American legend.

TRUTH AND HONESTY

WHAT DOES IT MEAN TO BE HONEST? One way to be an honest person is to tell the truth. A popular story American schoolchildren learn is about America's first president, George Washington. No one knows if this is a true story. But it is certainly a story about truth.

One day young George Washington's father was very angry. A young cherry tree he had planted had been chopped down.

"How did this happen?" he demanded. "Who would destroy this beautiful young tree? Do you know who did this, George?"

"I did, Father. I cannot tell a lie. I chopped it down with my new axe."

This story has appeared in books for children for many years after George Washington's death. We call it a legend. It is a story that has been told and retold many times. We could also call it a "tall tale." A tall tale tells what might be true by stretching the truth. Legends and tall tales aren't untrue, because they explain what is true. This story reminds us that George Washington was a great and honest man.

Another great American, Abraham Lincoln, was called "Honest Abe." He was known to be frank and fair, open and upright in all his dealings with people. Frank and fair, open and upright are listed in the definition of "honest" in some dictionaries. This is how a great American president got his nickname.

Does an honest person always tell the truth? That is a hard question to answer. Sometimes telling the truth can be painful or harmful to someone else. In a case like that, a person must be very thoughtful and careful. A doctor may have to think very long and hard before telling a patient, or a patient's family, some bad news.

Sometimes truth and honesty are not the same. The difference between truth and honesty can be the difference between stating a fact and expressing an opinion. An opinion is honest if you are saying something that you really believe. But a fact is true only if you can prove that it is true.

President Lincoln was known for his honesty and fairness.

Here are some true facts:

1) The earth takes a year to travel around the sun.

2) Bruce Springsteen recorded "Born in the U.S.A."

3) Canada and Mexico are neighbors of the United States.

Scientists have proven that the earth takes a year to travel around the sun. You can prove that Bruce Springsteen recorded "Born in the U.S.A." Show someone the record album on which he sings that song. You can see on a map that Canada borders on the United States to the north. And Mexico borders the U.S. on the south.

Here are some honest opinions:

1) The earth is the only planet that has people on it.

2) Bruce Springsteen is the greatest popular singer around today.

3) Canada is a great place to take a vacation.

An honest opinion is different from a fact. An honest opinion is sincere–the person who holds the opinion really believes it. But no one can *prove* that it is true.

Sometimes the Truth Really Matters

We know that people have been telling lies for at least 2,500 years. The following fable was first told at least that long ago. A fable is a story that ends with a message. The message is called the "moral." This fable is told by Aesop (Ee-sop). He was a Greek story-teller of long ago. His fables were all about human problems. That is why they have lasted all this time. The messages they teach are still important.

The Shepherd Who Cried "Wolf"

Each day, a young shepherd led his sheep to the hills not far from his village. While the sheep ate the grass, the shepherd had little to do.

One day, he thought of a trick to play on the villagers. He shouted, "Wolf! Help!" The villagers dropped whatever they were doing. They ran to the hills to help. The shepherd boy laughed and laughed when he saw them all come running.

It was such a good trick that the shepherd boy tried it again a few days later. "Wolf! Wolf! Help! Help!," he cried. The villagers thought that this time there must be a real wolf. They didn't believe the boy would play the same trick twice. Once more they ran to the hills to help. Once more, the shepherd boy was laughing. He laughed so hard he had to hold his sides to keep from hurting.

The following week, the wolf really did come to the hillside. The shepherd boy shouted as loud as he could, "Wolf!! Help!! Help!! Wolf!! Help my poor sheep!!" But this time the villagers did the laughing. They kept right on with their work. No one believed the shepherd boy any more.

The wolf killed many of the sheep. The horrified shepherd boy looked on. He learned his lesson the hard way. If one is to be believed, one must always tell the truth.

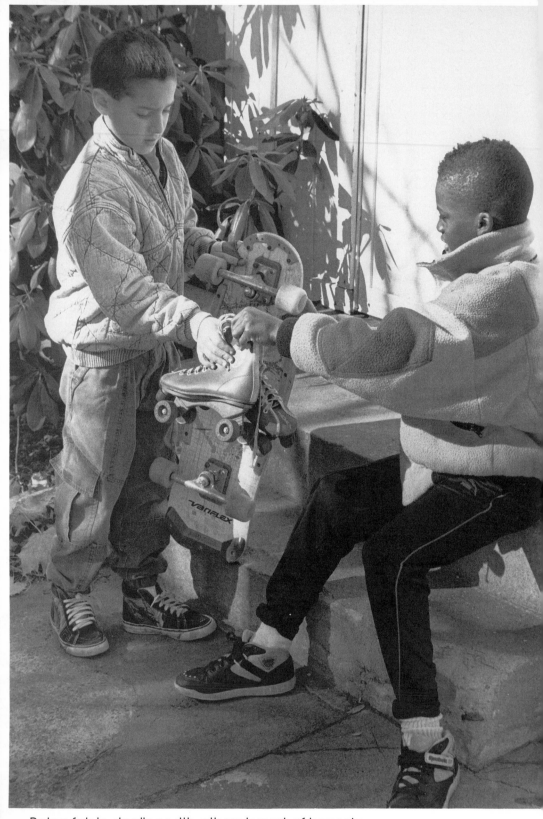

Being fair in dealing with others is part of honesty.

2

HONESTY IS THE BEST POLICY

BILL AND HUEY ARE GOOD FRIENDS. Last February they agreed to swap Bill's old skateboard for Huey's old pair of ice skates. They were both pleased. Each thought it was a fair and square trade. Bill didn't need *two* skateboards. Huey's skates were just the right size for Bill, but too small for Huey. Huey didn't have to squeeze into them any more. He had been given a new pair of skates for Christmas. The boys made the deal one day after school. There was a smooth, fresh layer of good, thick ice on the pond.

"C'mon. Let's get the skates and try out the ice." Huey started home at a run.

"Do you want to pick up the skateboard first?" Bill called.

"We have to wait for spring to go skateboarding. The pond could be a swampy mess by tomorrow." Huey started off again. Bill tried to keep up with him.

It was a great day for skating. Huey was a good teacher and Bill caught on quickly. It was almost five o'clock when they started home. They wanted to stop first at Bill's house. Huey wanted to pick up the skateboard. Bill had promised to give Huey a skateboard lesson the following morning. Both boys hoped it would be warmer then. They couldn't go skateboarding on icy streets.

Bill headed for his back porch and Huey followed. Bill had left the skateboard there the day before. He wanted to clean it up. And he wanted to add a few extra ball bearings to one set of wheels. But there was no skateboard on the back porch, just the set of shiny wheels. When he asked his mom, she didn't know. She said that she hired someone to clean up the junk in the backyard. Bill should look out there.

There was a fire burning in the trash basket. Most of the flames were licking at a skateboard.

Bill didn't say anything to Huey. He walked through the hall to the front door. Huey followed. Bill picked up his skates on the front porch and handed them back to Huey.

"What's up?," Huey asked.

"I don't have anything to trade." Bill said. "Dad gave me the new skateboard for my birthday. I can't trade that one away."

Huey looked at Bill. "It's *winter*," he said. "Who needs a skateboard now? Keep the skates, so we both have ice skates to use. We'll worry about skateboards when spring comes."

Bill ran to the back door again. "We gotta get that other set of wheels out of the trash basket before they melt! I'll have time to make a new board...Yeah."

This year, both Huey and Bill are on the Junior high school ice-skating team. Huey looks really cool on his "new" skateboard.

Huey understood that what had happened to the skateboard wasn't Bill's fault. He figured that the fair thing was for both of them to make the best of it, together.

Bill tried to return the skates to Huey. He told Huey right away why he couldn't give away his "birthday" skateboard. And he made good on his promise to make a new one. Huey and Bill were frank and fair with each other. They are still good friends.

No Talking

Do *you* know anyone who wants to be called dishonest? Does *anyone* want to be known as a liar or a cheat
or a thief? Probably not. Most of us try to be honest.
Sometimes it is hard to be honest. Let's look at what
happened in Ms. Quigley's classroom.

Ms. Quigley never allows talking during exams. In the
middle of the midterm math test, the whole class heard
Ms. Quigley call Barry Green to her desk.

"You were talking to Janet," she said. "You know the
rules. Hand in your test and leave the room."

"Yes, Ma'am. I'm sorry," Barry answered. He stood up
and gathered his papers together. He walked slowly up
the aisle toward her desk.

Janet jumped up. "*I* was talking," Janet explained.
"My pencil rolled under Barry's desk. *I* asked *him* to pick
it up. I was the one who was talking."

Who was telling the truth? Who was telling a lie?
Janet was being honest. She didn't want Barry to be
blamed for something she had done. Barry was being
dishonest.

What do you think? Why did Barry lie?

Did Ms. Quigley forgive Barry?

Sometimes we lie to protect someone. Sometimes
that's good. Sometimes it's not. If Janet hadn't spoken

The teacher counts on the student's honesty when taking an exam.

up, Barry would have been in trouble. But Janet would have been in trouble, too. She might have passed the math test, but not the test of friendship.

Suppose Barry had told the truth?

Suppose he had said, "I didn't talk, Janet spoke to me." What do you think would have happened then?

The Rivals

Maryanne and Eleanor had been "best friends" since second grade. They had always shared everything. But now, in high school, they liked the same boy. His name was Richard. They couldn't share him.

The two girls didn't have a fight. They just weren't talking to each other much.

One school night, Maryanne went to a movie with Richard. Richard had done a lot of talking on the way home. Now Maryanne had to do a lot of thinking.

Richard had been talking about Eleanor. He hadn't exactly said that they were "doing it." But he said that she was willing to have sex with him. He wanted to know if Maryanne wanted to do it. He told her he liked her better. But he would go steady with Eleanor if Maryanne wasn't ready for sex.

Maryanne told Richard she had to think about that. She wasn't sure about having sex.

Maryanne did a lot of thinking that night. First she got angry at Eleanor. She thought all kinds of mean thoughts about her. Then she thought about "going all the way" with Richard and all that it might mean. She could get pregnant. She and Richard were too young for marriage and kids. She wouldn't be able to go to college.

Most of all, Maryanne looked at how she felt about Richard. Was she really in love with him? Would she *want* to marry him, someday, even if she didn't have to? Or did she just want to take him away from Eleanor?

Maryanne tried to decide how Richard felt about her. Did he love her? Eleanor was very sexy-looking. Maryanne didn't have a chance against Eleanor in *that* department. Would Richard want to marry her even if he didn't have to? Not if he was using her and Eleanor against each other. She and Eleanor ought to have a talk.

In class the next day Maryanne slipped a note to Eleanor. It said:

See you after school. Usual place.

The two friends talked. It turned out that Eleanor had told Richard she was "ready" to *never see him again.* The two friends laughed and laughed and laughed.

Richard had not been honest with Maryanne. He had not been honest with Eleanor, either. He had lied to Maryanne about Eleanor. That's one kind of dishonesty.

True friends communicate honestly with each other.

He had lied in another way, too. He didn't have any true feelings for Maryanne or Eleanor. He was using them. He knew they liked him. He tried to use their feelings to get something he wanted. He was dishonest about his feelings for them.

Maryanne and Eleanor were lucky. They were true friends. They didn't let their feelings for Richard get in the way. Their honesty with each other helped them to stay good friends. And it helped them both to see that Richard was *not* honest.

Not sticking to your diet is a way of being dishonest with yourself.

3

BE HONEST WITH YOURSELF

THERE IS AN OLD SAYING, "Be true to yourself and you will not be false to others." "Well," you can say, "that's easy enough. I don't lie to myself. Why should I? There's no reason to." Right? Wrong. There are many reasons and many ways in which we lie to ourselves. Let's look at a few:

I won't forget...

One fudge sundae doesn't mean I'm off my diet...

I didn't *promise* I'd get home early, I just *said* I would...

I really need it...

I can't...

I'll clean up tomorrow...

I'll do it later...

Chapter Three

It was his fault...
She made me do it...
I didn't mean to...
I had to...
I didn't like him, anyhow...
I don't care...
Of course I care...
Who cares...
I'm sorry...
I'm not a bit sorry...
She'll be sorry.

These are the kinds of lies most of us tell ourselves.
You may remember a few of your own favorites. See if
you can get rid of some of them.

Maybe you are saying to yourself, "I really mean those
things when I say them. They are not really lies. That's
not being dishonest." But you know the difference. All
you have to do is think about it. How many "tomor-
rows," for example, does it take before you *do* clean your
room?

This kind of dishonesty doesn't hurt anyone but you.
Most of us tell many of these little lies to ourselves.
Learning to see them for what they are is part of growing
up. A responsible person doesn't have to lie to herself or
himself. She or he keeps promises.

If you promise to clean up your room, then you should keep your word and do it.

Do you think Abraham Lincoln and George Washington ever told themselves these kinds of "little" lies. Probably. As they grew up, though, they grew more and more honest on the inside. People like Washington and Lincoln are good examples for others. They were honest with themselves and with other people. They told the truth as they saw it. When they saw things that needed changing they told the truth. Then they worked to make those changes happen.

Many of the lies we tell ourselves aren't very bad. They can be comforting. But we should not use them too often. And we will be all right if we can "grow up." Then we can leave these kinds of lies behind.

But some lies are really dangerous. The more of these lies we tell ourselves the more dangerous they become. Especially if we begin to believe them.

Maybe you know someone like Tom Williams. Tom started telling himself lies very early in life. He didn't do well in junior high. He lied to himself about homework and good grades. He lied about being sick so he could stay home from school. Somehow he managed to scrape through final exams. He graduated with his class. In high school he began to tell himself even bigger lies:

It's only beer...

It's only wine...

It never affects me...

Lying to yourself about drugs and alcohol is both dishonest and dangerous.

I won't have more than one...
So, okay, I only had two...
Three? No way...
Sure I can drive...
I smoke maybe only five a week...
I'll just do it once...
Hooked? Me? Not me...
I can stop anytime...
I just like it...
I can handle it...
Quitting's easy...
Not just now...
Later... sure...

He'll never miss it...

I didn't...

She made me do it...

It wasn't my fault...

When you get in the habit of being dishonest with yourself, bad things can happen to you, and to others. What do you think happened to Tom Williams?

The No-Hit, No-Pitch Super-Star

It is hard to be honest with ourselves. But honesty can make a big difference in our lives.

Jim is a real baseball fan. He's a senior in high school. He has never missed a single high school baseball game. Back in eighth grade, he had managed to get on the junior high team. But he had been their worst player. They made jokes about him. "Jim? He can't even hit a ball—a basketball." "Him? When he's on the mound, batters wear their walking shoes." "He couldn't find home plate with a road sign." Jim had a weak right eye. It didn't affect his sight, because he wore glasses. But as a pitcher, he had a problem with his aim.

Jim had to admit to himself that he would never be a baseball star. "I have to be fair," Jim decided. "I won't even try out for the high school team. I'm no hitter, I'm no pitcher. All I'm good at is running bases. But I always strike out. So when do I get a chance to run? Running! Hey! I wonder if I could make it on the track team?"

These days Jim shows up at every baseball game–to cheer for the team. Everyone knows him. No one makes jokes about him anymore. He is the track team's super-star. He is also president of the student body, and was voted "most popular senior."

Jim admitted to himself that he wasn't good at baseball. Then things changed. He could see the things he *could* do well. And there were plenty of them. Being honest with yourself will always help. You will see things more clearly. The decisions you make about yourself will be good ones.

People can get hurt when a secret becomes gossip.

4

GOSSIPS, TATTLETALES AND LITTLE WHITE LIES

DO YOU EVER GOSSIP? *No? Are you sure? To gossip* means to talk about something, or someone, you know or you have heard about. You and your friends probably exchange this kind of information often. It may seem as if you are just having an interesting conversation. Gossip *is* often interesting. But it is also often *untrue*.

Did you ever play the "Whisper Game?" Try it. Eight or more people stand in a line. One person starts the game. He or she whispers a piece of information to the next person in line. Person two repeats what he or she hears to person three, and so on. Soon the message reaches the last person in the row. He or she repeats the message *out loud*. It is almost always a *different* message! Here's an example of what may happen:

Larry whispers to Ellen, "Jake keeps two sailboats by that leaky dock, near the library."

And Ellen whispers what she thinks she heard, to Christine. "Jake keeps a goat, with, I think he said, two tails, all week in some doctor's laboratory...."

Then Christine whispers to George, "Jake keeps a goat with two long, slinky tails and a beak in Dr. Sommers lavatory."

And so on. It is a funny game. But when you gossip about friends, it isn't so funny.

Without planning to, people who gossip often stretch the truth. When facts are repeated from one person to another, over and over, they change and change again. Soon they are no longer true at all.

Secrets

Did you ever swear to keep a secret that your best friend wanted to tell you? Who would keep a secret better than you? Of course, you didn't know how difficult that promise was going to be to keep. It was easy to promise *before you knew what an interesting secret it was!* Now, it isn't only your best friend who wants to tell someone – it's *you*, too. Maybe another very good friend of yours will swear, as you did, to keep the secret. But your very good friend has a good friend too. Once a secret is shared, it is no longer a secret. Very often, it becomes an interesting subject for *gossip*.

Most people who gossip don't mean to hurt anyone. They don't mean to hurt anyone's feelings. They just don't realize what can happen when the "truth" goes

Being honest about your abilities will help you be a winner.

through so many "hands" (mouths). No one who gossips means to be dishonest. But if gossip results in something untrue being told to others, that can be serious. Someone can be hurt. Someone's feelings can surely be hurt. The same thing can happen with secrets.

Be as honest as you can be with others. Try not to gossip. If someone tells you gossip, let them know you

understand what gossip is. Don't tempt your friends to
gossip by telling "secrets." And if someone wants to tell
you a secret, think hard. Be sure you can keep it a secret.
Or be honest, and admit that secrets are really hard to
keep.

Tattletales

In elementary school there is almost always one kid in
class who is the "teacher's pet." He or she is not very
popular. That is because one of the ways they help the
teacher is to *tattle*. They tell the teacher everything that
goes on in the classroom. So most teacher's pets are also
called tattletales.

The word tattletale isn't used much when you get
older. New, tougher words that mean the same thing take
its place: rat, squealer, blab, snitch, and other names.
Whatever word you use, telling on someone, or telling
about something you know to be true, needs thinking
about. It's a matter of purpose. *Why* you tell is almost as
important as *what* you tell.

Paul was a new kid in Arlene's class. He seemed to be
a loner. He made no effort to make friends. He had
arrived in the middle of the school term. Since then there
had been more practical jokes than usual played in the

classroom. No one knew who the joker was. No one suspected Paul.

One morning Arlene came to class early. She wanted to finish a paper she had to hand in. When she opened the door, she saw Paul at the teacher's desk. He was putting something into the teacher's desk drawer.

That something turned out to be a toy mouse. It looked real enough to scare anyone who was even a little afraid of mice. Arlene could have reported this. Paul would have been in serious trouble. But she decided to get him to take the mouse out of the drawer. She talked with him about making friends in class. She tried to tell him there were better ways of getting attention.

For several weeks, there were no more practical jokes. Arlene smiled at Paul when she saw him in the hall or in class. Paul began spending time with some other kids in the class. They were not the greatest guys to have for friends, Arlene thought. But at least Paul had stopped being a loner. Now Paul hardly ever returned her smile. She wasn't happy about that. But she ignored it.

Soon Arlene had to make another decision about Paul. She had started for home one day and left her books in the classroom. Mr. Colby, the gym teacher, was just leaving. He didn't want her to go up to the fourth floor alone. They started up the stairs. Making the turn on the

If someone was hurt as a result of a "practical joke," would you tell?

second floor landing, they heard someone on the third.

Whoever it was took off. All they saw were socks and sneakers running away. A ball of thin, strong cord rolled down to them. When they reached the third floor landing, they saw that the cord had been wrapped several times around the upright stair rails on each side of the second step. When tightened and tied, it would have been a perfect way to trip someone. There would have been a serious accident.

Mr. Colby removed the cord and rewound it.

"We have to find that kid," he said. "But it won't be easy."

Arlene was very quiet. She had to decide what to do. "Why do you think he was doing that," she asked. "Do you think he really wanted to hurt somebody – just anybody?"

"Why did you say *he*," Mr. Colby asked. "Those sneakers could just as easily belong to a girl."

"Because I know who he is. He was in class today. He was wearing those same dirty white sneakers with the green shoe laces. And the same yellow and black striped socks. He needs to talk to someone who will know how to help him. I think he should see a guidance counselor."

Arlene told Mr. Colby that she thought Paul had tied that cord on the stairs. Her purpose was honest and kind and intelligent. It was clear that Paul needed help. He didn't know how seriously someone could be hurt by that kind of a "joke."

Those Little White Lies

"I'd love to go to the movies with you, Chuck. But I promised Mom I'd stay home and help her tonight." Ginny hung up the phone, yanked on a sweater, and started for the front door. "Where are you going, Ginny?"

Mom asked. "Next door. To Ellen's. I'll be back in an hour. If I go to bed early, I'll stay on my diet. Listen, if Chuck calls again, tell him I'm helping you. Tell him that I can't come to the phone. Okay?"

"Guess so. I heard you turn him down. But why did you lie? Why not just say you didn't feel like going out?"

"I didn't feel like going out with *him*, Mom. He's sweet but he's too young. Why hurt his feelings? It was just a white lie."

Have you ever told a white lie? Is that a bad thing to do? It depends on why you did it.

Ginny knows that Chuck has a crush on her. But he's fifteen. He's just a kid. Ginny is almost seventeen. She wants to date someone older than she is. So Ginny tells a white lie. She should have thought about what she was doing. She would have realized something. In the long run her white lie wasn't going to help. Chuck will probably try to date her again and again. And each time he tries, Ginny will have to dream up a new reason for saying "No."

It will become harder and harder for Chuck to make himself believe her. He will get her message, but slowly and painfully. Ginny told Chuck a white lie because she wanted to be nice to him. Honesty would have been kinder.

There may be times when telling a white lie is the right

thing to do. A white lie can be kind when its purpose is kind.

Pete and Alice live in the same building. They have known each other since Alice hit Pete over the head with her shovel in the sandbox. They have been friends all through school. They treat each other like brother and sister. Now they are in high school and they share the same friends.

A while ago Pete had a crush on Marilyn, one of Alice's friends. He had that miserable, sure feeling that Marilyn didn't like him — not even a little bit.

Alice was sitting on the stoop by herself one day when Pete got home. "Listen, Allie," he said, "You oughta know. Why doesn't Marilyn give me a break? Do I have bad breath or what?"

Alice knew how Marilyn felt about Pete. Marilyn, as a matter of fact, had just given Alice her opinion of Pete. "He's a real nerd," she had said.

Alice smiled at Pete. "She's weird," Alice said. "She thinks you're a real serious type. You're too serious for her."

Alice's purpose was to be kind, and she was. She let Pete know he wasn't Marilyn's type. But she made Pete feel that he didn't need to take it as a put-down. Alice is a good friend to Pete. And she is a good friend to Marilyn, too.

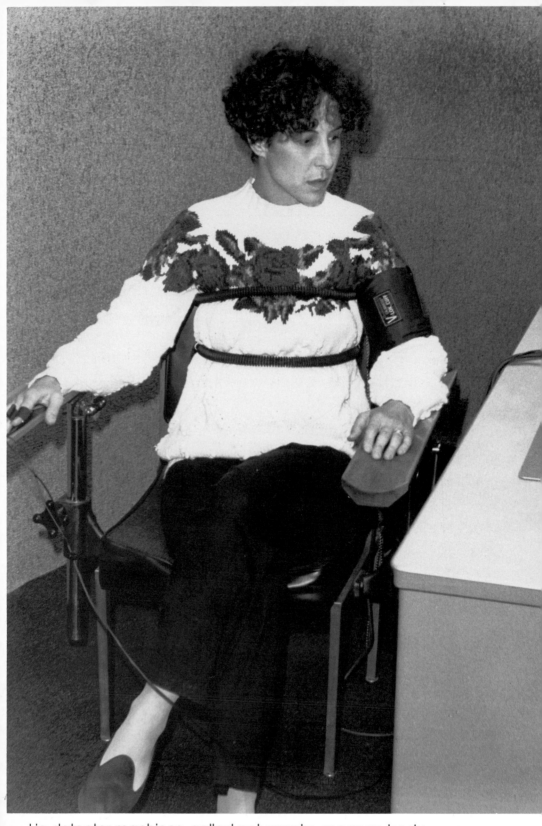
Lie-detector machines, called polygraphs, measure body
changes that can show if a person is not telling the truth.

5

HONESTY AT WORK

UP TO NOW WE HAVE TALKED ABOUT *PERSONAL* HONESTY. We
discussed honesty and truth. We looked at being honest
with ourselves. We talked about being honest with others.

Other reasons for honesty come up in the real world.
Honesty is important to preserve order under the law.
Police and other law enforcement people need to be able
to judge a person's honesty.

We are still looking for the perfect test. For thousands
of years, "truth-tests" were very painful. Sometimes they
were fatal. Most of the "tests" were based on the idea that
a person was innocent only if they were still alive after
many dreadful hours of "testing." The judges were usu-
ally quite certain that the "accused" had been guilty. So
people thought that deaths caused by the tests proved

that the "guilty" had been fairly punished for their sins. Today we understand that such tests were really torture. They had very little to do with truth or honesty.

There is still no foolproof method of testing for honesty. But we are closer to finding one.

The first lie-dector machine was invented in 1895. It seemed to show that lying caused a quick change in blood pressure. Its inventors believed that even though there was no outward sign, the machine could tell. As soon as the tested person lied, the blood began moving faster through the body. Then the blood pressure rose. The machine measured the change.

Today's lie-detector machine (*polygraph*) is much more complex. It *graphs* (draws charts of) a number of body activities: blood pressure, pulse (or heartbeat), breathing, and perspiration. Those who believe in it claim that the graphs show the difference between true and false answers.

Different states have different rules about using a polygraph in court. But even when it can't be used to prove guilt or innocence, a polygraph test may be used. A defense lawyer may use a polygraph. He or she will try to show that an accused person *may* be innocent.

A person accused of a crime may ask to take a lie detector test. The person expects the machine to show that he or she is innocent.

If you have a job, you
have a responsibility to be
honest.

Sometimes criminals ask to be tested. They think they can "beat the machine." They often learn that their lies have been discovered. Polygraphs have even helped to get confessions. People tell the truth because the machine has caught their lies.

The polygraph is still not totally accepted. Many people believe that the machine could be a "false witness." They argue that something important is still in question. It has never been proven that the changes in body activities shown by the machine are produced only when a person tells a lie. Some people also think this test is an abuse of civil rights. In one way, however, the polygraph is better than the truth-tests of the past. No physical pain is involved in a polygraph test.

Keeping Business Honest

Many government agencies and services exist to keep people safe and honest. And almost every federal department and agency has a section that deals with honesty and the law. The U.S. Postal Service is always looking for criminals who use the mails to trick and rob people. Have you ever read an ad that sounded too good to be true? It probably was! As soon as someone complains, the Postal Service investigators go to work. They try to find and arrest the crooks. And they have a high rate of

The Food and Drug Administration (FDA) makes sure that drug companies produce safe products.

success. They solve crimes that involve many millions of dollars.

The Treasury Department has its own investigators. So do the U.S. Customs Service and the Immigration Services.

The FDA (Food and Drug Administration) is concerned with keeping us healthy. The FDA investigators, or detectives, are mainly scientists. They test every new medicine to make sure that it is safe. The FDA makes sure that the drug companies give *honest* information to consumers about their products. They have to approve every drug before it can be sold to the public. They also test mouthwashes, toothpastes, and insecticides. They test any product that might be dangerous in the home.

The FDA also watches the food industry. They make sure that the labels on canned, frozen, and packaged foods are complete and honest. Food producers must, by law, name all the ingredients, including chemicals, that go into the food. They must print a list on the can or package label for the consumer's information. And the honest weight of the product must be printed on the wrapping. No one can sell a half pound of rice in a pound-size box and get away with it.

The FCC (Federal Communications Commission) deals with honesty in advertising. They keep track of newspapers and magazines, television, radio and all other ways

Food labels must contain
a full list of ingredients.

we get information. The Office of the Surgeon General is the watchdog agency for our national health. That office deals with the need for truth and honesty about AIDS, cancer-causing tobacco, alcohol and other drugs.

The EPA (Environmental Protection Agency) studies methods of keeping the world clean enough for people and animals to live in. They study things that are dangerous to life on earth. Auto fumes, oil spills, acid rain, nuclear accidents and other little and big disasters can occur. EPA tries to learn the truth so that they can do what is necessary. They try to prevent dangerous things from happening again.

There are many more government agencies, each looking for honest answers in their own special area.

6

ARE YOU AN HONEST PERSON?

A **NATIONAL TELEVISION NEWS MAGAZINE PROGRAM** did a story on personal honesty. It showed some experiments. The experiments were based on incidents that had happened in real life. Teams with cameras were sent to several American cities and towns. The program showed what happened.

In one experiment, an armored truck stopped in a shopping mall parking lot. On the way out, the truck dropped an open bag of one-dollar bills out a back door. The money fell out of the bag onto the ground. The cameras recorded some people picking up handfuls of the money as they passed by. Some took only a small

If you received too much change at the supermarket, would you return it?

amount. Others stuffed their pockets or shopping bags with one-dollar bills. Others did not take any of the money. They simply walked away. Some people told other people what had happened.

After a while, someone was sent to the parking lot to ask for the money back. At first it seemed that most people who had taken the money were willing to give it back. The crew collected what they thought was a lot of the money. But when it was counted, the program reported, only about 440 of the 1,000 one-dollar bills had been returned.

This experiment was based on some real-life incidents. Often a bag of money has fallen off a truck onto a highway. Once, a man found hundreds of thousands of dollars–and turned all of it in to the police. He was rewarded very generously. Ten percent of the money he returned was his reward. The man received many thousands of dollars for his honesty. But he had not returned the money to get a reward. He had returned it because he believed it would be wrong to keep something that didn't belong to him. Other people must have found the rest of the money. But no one else reported the incident.

In another case, most of the money that fell off of a truck was never recovered. Many thousands of dollars simply disappeared. It was taken from the lanes of a major highway somewhere in the American Midwest.

Another experiment was done in several cities. Each time, a camera crew left a wallet on a sidewalk. Then they filmed what happened as people walked by.

One wallet was found by a group of young men. They picked it up and went right into a bar. Another young person saw the wallet, bent down, picked it up and kept on walking. One young man picked up the wallet and ran after the man who dropped it. Another person picked up the wallet and walked into the nearest building. She turned it over to the security guard.

There were two more experiments. They were the same, except for the kind of place they were conducted in. In both cases, people were given too much change when they made a purchase in a store.

In one experiment, camera crews were hidden in a shop that belonged to a national chain of stores. In another, cameras were hidden in a small store owned by a local merchant. The result was very interesting.

Many people in both stores immediately gave back the "extra" money. But many more people kept the "extra" money they received in the chain store. Most of the people who got too much change from the local merchant's store gave it back and told the clerk. This shows that people seemed to care more about being honest when the situation was more personal.

After the filmed report, the program presented a short

If you do not tell the truth
on a job application, you
can be fired later on.

test that people at home could take. The answers to the test questions can be used to judge someone's honesty. Here are some questions like the ones on the program. Take the test. You don't really need an answer key to figure out how honest you are.

How Honest Are You?

1. You see someone drop a wallet on the street in front of you. Would you run after the person to give it back?

2. You see a wallet on the street. You pick it up. It has almost a hundred dollars in it. It also has an ID card with the owner's address and phone number. What would you do? Would you return the wallet AND the money? Would you keep the money and return the wallet? Would you take the money and throw the wallet away?

3. You see a wallet on the street. You pick it up. It has a few dollars in it, some photos and other personal stuff. But there is no ID. Would you keep the money and throw the other stuff away? Would you turn everything over to the police? Would you keep the money and turn the rest of it in to the police?

4. Would *you* keep money that you found behind the open door of an armored truck? Would *you* keep money that fell out of a truck onto the highway?

5. You go into an ice cream shop for a treat. You pay for a 95-cent ice cream cone with a dollar. The clerk gives

you change for a ten-dollar bill. Do you tell the clerk he has made a mistake and give the extra money back to him?

6. You are applying for a job. To get the job you have to have experience using a word processor. You don't have the experience, but you really want the job. Would you say you have the experience anyway?

7. You want to date someone in a higher grade than you are in school. Would you lie about your school grade and your age to get a date?

8. You are being punished for getting a bad report card. You cannot go anywhere after school. Someone you really like asks you out for pizza. They never asked you out before. Would you tell your friend the truth and suggest a date some time in the future?

9. One of your friends got a new haircut. You don't think it looks good. Your friend is unsure about his new look. He asks your opinion. What will you say?

Some of these questions are not easy to answer. Some of the situations are serious. Some are less so. In at least one case, being honest would mean being unkind. This test shows that how honest you are is not always a simple issue.

You can be honest about a friend's haircut without being unkind. But you have to be thoughtful. You can say, "I really liked the haircut you had before. This is

A lost wallet filled with money is tempting to keep. How many people would return it?

very different." You have said things you really believe. And you have not said anything that might hurt your friend's feelings.

Being honest about something you don't want others to know is a little harder. Sometimes it will do no harm if you do not tell the *whole* truth. You can tell someone you can't go out after school. You do not have to say why.

Some of the other issues are more difficult. If you lie on a job application, for example, it may do you more harm than good. If you get the job but don't have the skills to perform, it will be hard to keep it. And your employer will probably not think well of you when he knows that you were dishonest. It is better to say, "I don't have word processing skills," for example, "but I really want to learn." You may get an opportunity that way.

The other issues are clearer. But the decisions are still not very easy ones. Money is very tempting, especially when it doesn't clearly belong to anyone you know or can see. You don't know the owner of the 300 "Delicious Donut" shops, for example. How much will such a big business miss a few dollars? But most of the time this kind of mistake is made, the clerk will be the loser. If the cash drawer is short, the money will often come out of an employee's pay. If you had a job selling ice cream, and you made a mistake, how would you feel? Suppose you gave someone nine dollars too much change and you had to pay the money back. You would have to work for almost three hours without pay to make it up. You could even lose a job for making this kind of a mistake, if it cost the company a lot of money. Your answer may be different if you look at the question a little more personally.

Giving back money to a bank seems very different to many people. But it would be hard to enjoy money like that if you kept a lot of it. It is against the law not to pay taxes on income. It is hard to spend money if you can't explain where it came from. Believe it or not, honesty is really "the best policy."

Glossary: *Explaining New Words*

dishonest Lacking in honesty, untrustworthy.

exaggerate Overstate; make something seem bigger or better than it is.

fable A story that teaches a moral.

fact Truth; reality.

FCC The Federal Communications Comission, which keeps track of honesty in advertising.

FDA The Food and Drug Administration, which tests new products to make sure that they are safe to use and that their labels are honest about their contents.

frank Open or straightforward; sincere in expression.

gossip Rumors of a personal nature; casual talk.

honest Truthful; not lying, cheating, stealing, or taking unfair advantage; real or genuine.

honorable Having integrity and deserving respect.

integrity Belief in and willingness to live by a code of values.

legend A popular story, handed down from the past, that cannot be proved true.

lie detector (polygraph) Machine used to detect lying by measuring physical signs such as pulse or breathing when questions are asked.

moral A principle or idea that a person lives by.

opinion A belief that cannot be proven by facts.

perjury Telling a lie after swearing to tell only the truth.

For Further Reading

Colman, Hila Crayder. *Confession of a Storyteller.* New York: Crown Publishers, Inc.,1981. A discussion of being honest in relationships with others.

Hughes, Dean. *Honestly, Myron.* New York: Atheneum Publishers,1982. Discusses the importance of communication and the two sides of insisting on absolute honesty.

Lorimar, Lawrence T. *Secrets.* New York: Holt, Rinehart and Winston, Inc.,1981. A sixteen-year-old tells her story. It is about her mixed feelings toward her parents and how she ends up dealing with her father's suicide.

For Further Reading

Perl, Lila. *Don't Ask Miranda*. New York: The Seabury Press, Inc.,1979. The discovery that friendship must be earned honestly is made by a young girl.

Sirof, Harriet. *Save the Dam!*. New York: Crestwood House, Inc.,1981. A story about the importance of sticking to the truth.

Shura, Mary Francis Craig. *The Barkley Street Six-pack*. New York: Dodd, Mead and Co., Inc.,1979. A young girl learns the truth about herself and her less-than-true friend.

INDEX

A

Aesop, 12

B

be(ing) honest with yourself,
  25-31

C

Customs Service (U.S.), 48

E

Environmental Protection Agency
  (EPA), 50

F

Federal Communications Com-
  mission (FCC), 48
Food and Drug Administration
  (FDA), 47, 48, 49

G

gossip, 33-36

H

honesty
  definition of, 6, 7, 10
  test of, 56-57

I

Immigration Services (U.S.), 48

L

lie(s)
  detector (polygraph), 42, 44,
    46
  "little white," 39-41
Lincoln, Abraham, 10-11, 28

O

Office of the Surgeon General
  (U.S.), 48, 50

P

perjury, definition of, 7
polygraph (lie dector), 42, 44,
  46
Postal Service (U.S.), 46, 48
practical jokes, 37-39

S

Shepherd Who Cried Wolf, The,
  14-15
Springsteen, Bruce, 11, 12

Index

Surgeon General (U.S.), Office
of the, 48, 59

T
tattletales, 36-38
Treasury Department, U.S., 48

U
U.S. Customs Service, 48
U.S. Postal Service, 46, 48

W
Washington, George, 8, 9-10, 28

About the Author

Vana Earle began her publishing career as author/illustrator of children's books. She has written, edited and designed text and trade books, a monthly news journal for young adults, as well as many stories and articles.

Photo Credits and Acknowledgments

Cover Photo: Charles Waldron
Pages 14,19,22,24,27,29,32,35,38,42,45,47,49,52,55,58, Stuart Rabinowitz; p.8,11, Culver Pictures Inc.

Design and Production: Blackbirch Graphics,Inc.